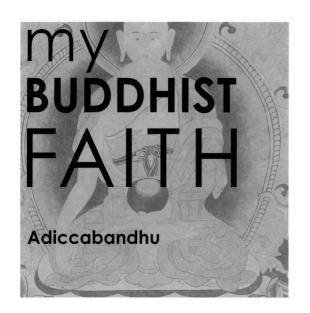

my BUDDHIST FAITH

Adiccabandhu

Evans

Contents

Notes for Teachers and Parents

Pages 6/7 The name Pramodya (pronounced Pram- O-jah) means 'joy'. In Buddhism, joy arises as a result of faith, or confidence. Buddhism began about 2,500 years ago in north-east India. Its teaching gradually spread across Asia, to such countries as Thailand, Burma, Sri Lanka, Cambodia, China, Japan and Tibet. At one time, a third of the world's population was Buddhist. As it took root in each new culture, it continued to develop. About 100 years ago, Buddhism spread to the West. All of the major eastern traditions are now established here, along with new Western schools. There are about 300 million Buddhists worldwide.

Pages 8/9/10 Even though Buddhists worship the Buddha, they do not regard him as a god. In fact, Buddhists do not have a creator god. They see the Buddha not as an ordinary human being, but as an Enlightened being, who perfected the human state. This state of perfection is also referred to as Nirvana or Nibbana. The word Buddha means 'The One who is Awake'. Although he is said to have perfected many wonderful virtues, the twin qualities of wisdom and compassion are regarded as of supreme importance. On pages 8, 9 and 10, Pramodya is making the three traditional offerings: flowers, candles and incense. Flowers make the shrine beautiful. They are also a reminder of the central Buddhist teaching that all things change. Candles symbolise the Buddha's wisdom lighting up the darkness of ignorance. The incense represents the positive effect that good actions have in the world.

Pages 11/12/13 The story of the Buddha's life is taken as the model for all who wish to tread the path to Enlightenment. Prince Siddattha (or Siddhartha) was born into the ruling family of a warrior caste. The legendary accounts say that a wise old man foretold that Siddattha would either be a great king or become a great holy man. The king tried to protect Siddattha from any signs of suffering. He did not want his son to become a holy man of the forest. The Buddha himself said he was spoiled, with all his desires fulfilled. He had a mansion for each of the three seasons.

Pages 13/ 14/15 Siddattha grew to manhood within the confines of the palace. He married the beautiful princess Yashodara and had a son called Rahula. Although he had everything he could wish for, he was still unhappy. He went out into the city in his chariot, and there saw the Four Sights that changed the course of his life. On four separate visits he encountered old age, sickness, death and a wandering holy man. Some of these sights are shown in the picture on page 13. His response was the Going Forth. He left home in order to find the answer to human suffering.

Pages 15/16/17 He spent many years wandering in the jungle, learning from the spiritual masters of the time. He then tried a life of extreme asceticism, but he still felt no nearer to the truth. Deciding that there must be a Middle Way between luxury and asceticism, he sat under a tree and meditated. He vowed he would not rise from the spot until he had found the truth. At last, he knew he had achieved his quest. He achieved a direct vision into the nature of reality. He had become a Buddha. The Buddha spent the remaining forty years of his life wandering the roads of north-east India, teaching people from all walks of life.

Pages 17/18/19/20 The Dhamma (or Dharma), the teaching of the Buddha, is essentially a path for those who wish to gain Enlightenment. The Dhamma also means the Truth. The first stage of the path is to try to live by the Five Precepts, which are all based on the principle of non-harm to self or others. The precepts are undertaken voluntarily by Buddhists. Each precept has a positive counterpart, a quality to be developed.

The Five Precepts: **1.** To avoid harming living beings and instead to practise helping others. **2.** To avoid stealing and instead to practise being generous. **3.** To avoid hurting others through being greedy and instead to practise contentment (this precept deals specifically with sexual misconduct). **4.** To avoid telling lies and instead to practise truthful speech. **5.** To avoid taking alcohol or drugs (for recreational use) and instead to keep the mind clear.

Pages 21/22/23 Many Buddhists meditate at home every day. They follow the movement of the breath as it goes in and out. This meditation leads to calmness. Another meditation helps develop loving kindness. Buddhists also like to meditate, study and worship together. The practice of gathering together helps strengthen the Sangha. The Sangha is the community of all those who follow the Buddha's teaching. For Buddhists the three most important things in life are the Triple Gem or Three Jewels: The Buddha, the Dhamma and the Sangha. Traditional offerings are flowers, candles and incense.

Pages 24/25 Monks and nuns belong to the monastic Sangha. The different monastic traditions or schools have different coloured robes. The monks of the Theravada tradition wear orange robes, while Tibetan monks and nuns wear purple robes. Monks, nuns and priests from the Chinese and Japanese schools of Buddhism usually wear black, grey or brown kimonos. Some Buddhist traditions have married priests. Schools will vary in their monastic rules, scriptures, styles of worship and festival days.

Pages 26/27 In Buddhism, ordination marks a commitment to have the Three Jewels at the centre of one's life. It is a Going Forth like that of Prince Siddattha. Marked by the taking of vows and the adoption of a new name, ordination is a commitment to practice, rather than the adoption of a particular lifestyle or ministerial role. In most traditions, as in the Theravada, this involves a monastic, celibate lifestyle. Others may follow a hermit's life, while still others may live in cities, more actively engaged in the world. Many ordained Buddhists wear a simple kesa, which represents the belt of the monastic robe. Members of the Buddhist Sangha try to help each other in whatever way they can.

Pages 28/29 The most widely celebrated festival is Wesak, which marks the Enlightenment of the Buddha. It is held on the full moon night of the months of May/June, when the Buddha is said to have gained Enlightenment. On festival days and other ceremonies, Buddhists chant a homage to the Triple Gem, or Three Jewels, and recite the Five Precepts as a renewal of their commitment to following the path to Enlightenment. This commitment is what makes them Buddhists, makes them members of the Sangha. The Sangha flourishes on friendship. The Buddha advised that friendship was the whole of the spiritual life. Generosity, kindly speech, encouragement and good example have been the traditional means by which friends in the Sangha have helped each other grow and develop. The lotus reminds Buddhists that everybody has the potential to grow and change, just as the lotus flower grows up through water towards the light.

My name is Pramodya.
I am a Buddhist.

Buddhists follow the
teaching of the **Buddha**.
We have a statue of the
Buddha on our home shrine.

Who was the Buddha?

The Buddha was a very wise man.
His teaching lit up the way
for us to follow.

When we light candles we remember how wise the Buddha was.

What are you lighting now?

I am lighting incense.
The sweet smell of incense helps us to remember how kind the Buddha was.

My dad often tells me the
story of the Buddha.
The Buddha was once a prince.
His name was **Siddattha Gotama.**

Prince Siddattha lived in India.
He lived in a beautiful palace.
One day, Prince Siddattha left
the palace.

12

He rode in a chariot.
He saw many people who
were unhappy.

He wanted to help, but he didn't
know what to do.

Siddattha went on a long journey.
He wanted to find out why there was
unhappiness in the world.

Nobody could tell him the answer.

After many years Siddattha decided to **meditate.**

He sat quietly under a tree.
At last he found the answer.

What did he do next?

He taught others how to find the answer too. People called him the Buddha, which means 'The One who is Awake'.

What did the Buddha teach?

The Buddha taught five guidelines for living, called **precepts.** My dad helps me to learn the precepts.

**Do you follow
the precepts?**

Yes. I try not to
hurt others,
or upset them.
Instead, I try to be
more kind to
people and
animals.

I try not to take what does not belong to me. Instead I try to share more.

I try not to tell lies.
Instead I try to tell the
truth, even when I don't
really want to.

What are you doing here?

I am learning to meditate. Mum and I sit very still and quiet. It helps us to be better people.

We worship at home and in the temple.

We chant and make offerings.

Buddhists belong to the Sangha.

The Sangha is like one big
world-wide family.

Do Buddhists have special clothes?

Some Buddhist monks and nuns shave their heads and wear robes, just like the Buddha did long ago.

These monks live in a **monastery** in Burma.
They study the Buddha's teachings and they meditate.

What is happening here?

My friend Padmasri is being **ordained**. She promises to follow the Buddha's teaching. She wears a kesa round her neck. It is like the monks' belt.

Padmasri helps me to learn about being a Buddhist. I try to help her, too.

We celebrate **Wesak** Day in May. On this day long ago, the Buddha found the answer to all his questions. It is called his **Enlightenment.**

28

Are friends important to Buddhists?

Yes! Friends help each other to be better people. Being kind and generous is especially important. I would like to be a good friend.

Glossary

Buddha - The founder of Buddhism. The word Buddha means 'The One who is Awake'.

Enlightenment - A state of perfect wisdom and kindness.

Gotama - The family name of Siddattha who became the Buddha.

Meditate - To make the mind calm and still.

Monastery - Place where monks and nuns live.

Ordained - Made a member of a religious order.

Precepts - Guidelines or rules for living followed by Buddhists.

Siddattha - The prince who became the Buddha.

Wesak - One of the names for the festival of the Buddha.

Index

Malpas   14.08.18